PIANO · VOCAL · GUITAR

The JERRY BOCK Songbook

ISBN 978-1-4584-1200-3

HAL•LEONARD® CORPORATION

7777 W. BLUEMOUND RD. P.O. BOX 13819 MILWAUKEE, WI 53213

Visit Hal Leonard Online at
www.halleonard.com

JERRY BOCK

BOCK, Jerry (Jerrold Lewis), composer; born New Haven, November 23, 1928; died November 2, 2010; son of George Joseph and Rebecca (Alpert) B.; married Patricia Faggen, May 28, 1950; children: George Albert, Portia Fane. Student, University of Wisconsin (1945–49), L.H.D. (hon.), 1985. Writer: score for high school musical, *My Dream*, 1943; score for college musical, *Big as Life*, 1948; songs for TV show "Admiral Broadway Revue," and "Show of Shows," 1949–51; composer songs, Camp Tamiment, summers 1950, 51, 53; writer: continuity sketches, "Mel Torme Show," CBS, 1951, 52; writing staff: "Kate Smith Hour," 1953–54; writer: original songs for night club performers, including night club revue, *Confetti*; wrote: songs for *Wonders of Manhattan* (honorable mention, Cannes Film Festival, 1956); composer: music for Broadway show, *Catch a Star*, 1955; *Mr. Wonderful*, 1956; (collaborated with Sheldon Harnick on) *The Body Beautiful*, 1958; *Fiorello!*, 1959 (Pulitzer prize, Drama Critics award, Antoinette Perry award); *Tenderloin*, 1960; *She Loves Me*, 1963; *Fiddler on the Roof*, 1964; *The Apple Tree*, 1966; *The Rothschilds*, 1972; London production of *She Loves Me*, 1964, off-Broadway 1982; *Fiddler on the Roof*, 1964 (nine Tonys® including Best Musical); London production of *Fiddler on the Roof*, 1964 (Tony® Award); Warsaw production, 1985, *Fiorello!*, Goodspeed Opera House, summer 1985; wrote series of children's songs now published under the title *Sing Something Special*; also recorded album, N.Y. Board of Education, radio broadcasts, 1961. Recipient Johnny Mercer award Songwriters Hall of Fame, 1990; named to Theatre Hall of Fame, 1990. Member Broadcast Music Inc. 1989–1990—Silver Anniversary production of *Fiddler on the Roof* National Tour, ending in New York Revival; 1989— Jerome Robbins' *Broadway*; 1990 —*The Rothschilds* revival. Member of an endowment group at the National Foundation for Advancement in the Arts. Member of the advisory panel for the BMI Foundation. Composed the score for the film, *A Stranger Among Us*; wrote words and music for *The Magic Journey, Danny and the Dragon, Brandon Finds His Star, Pinocchio* and *Land of Broken Toys* for the Children's Theatre Festival, University of Houston, 2000–2003.

DEAR FRIEND

from SHE LOVES ME

Words by SHELDON HARNICK
Music by JERRY BOCK

Poignantly (slowly)

pp

AMALIA:

Charm-ing, ro-man-tic, the per-fect ca-fé.

Then as if it is-n't bad e-nough, a vi-o-lin starts to play.

Can-dles and wine, ta-bles for two,

but where are you, dear friend?

cou - ples go past me, I see how they look.

So dis-creet-ly sym - pa - thet - ic when they see the rose and the book.

I make be - lieve, noth - ing is wrong.

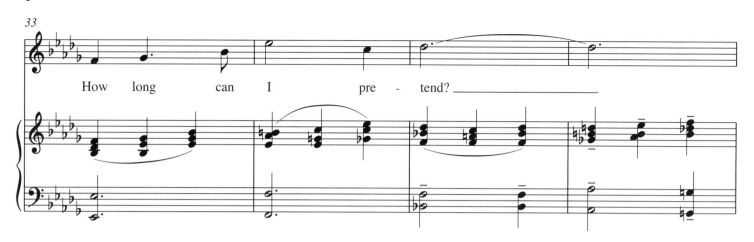

How long can I pre - tend? _____

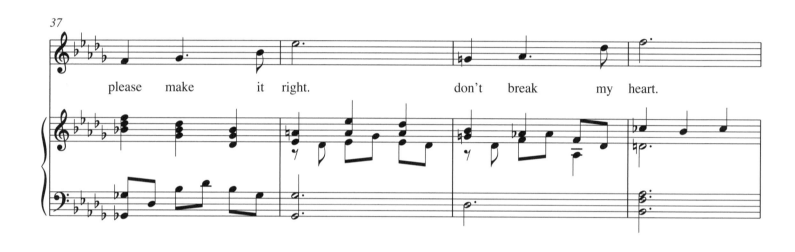

please make it right. don't break my heart.

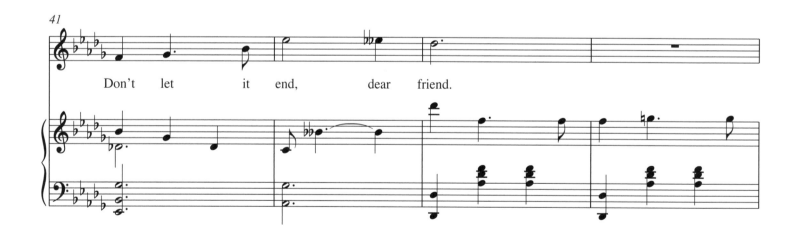

Don't let it end, dear friend.

FAR FROM THE HOME I LOVE

from the Musical FIDDLER ON THE ROOF

Words by SHELDON HARNICK
Music by JERRY BOCK

FEELINGS
from THE APPLE TREE

Words and Music by JERRY BOCK
and SHELDON HARNICK

FIDDLER ON THE ROOF
from the Musical FIDDLER ON THE ROOF

Words by SHELDON HARNICK
Music by JERRY BOCK

A - way a - bove my head I
un - ex - pect - ed breeze I could

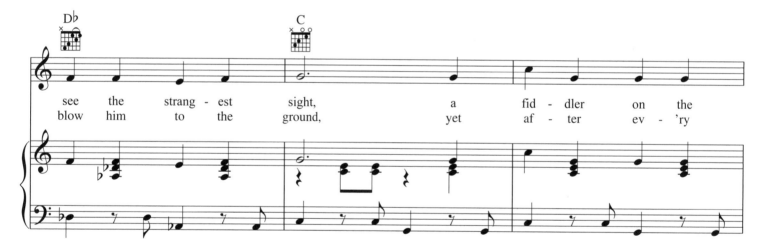

see the strang - est sight, a fid - dler on the
blow him to the ground, yet af - ter ev - 'ry

roof, who's up there day and night. He
storm, I see he's still a - round. What -

MR. WONDERFUL
from the Musical MR. WONDERFUL

Words and Music by JERRY BOCK,
LARRY HOLOFCENER and GEORGE WEISS

Slowly and expressively

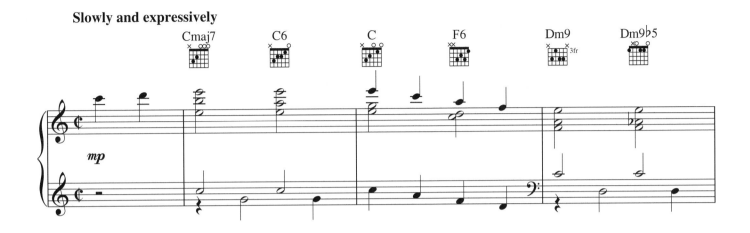

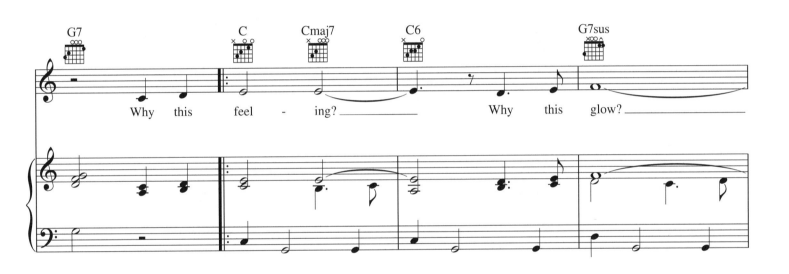

Why this feel - ing? _____ Why this glow? _____

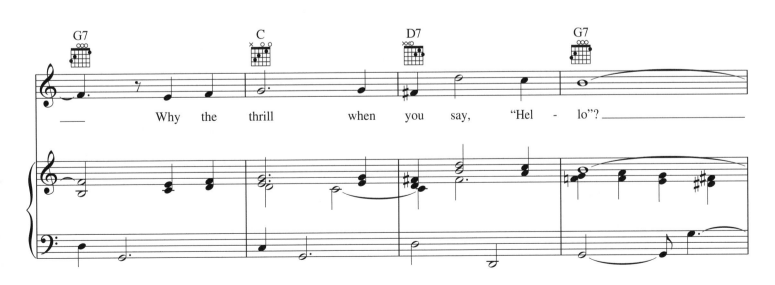

_____ Why the thrill when you say, "Hel - lo"? _____

IF I WERE A RICH MAN
from the Musical FIDDLER ON THE ROOF

Words by SHELDON HARNICK
Music by JERRY BOCK

26

MATCHMAKER

from the Musical FIDDLER ON THE ROOF

Words by SHELDON HARNICK
Music by JERRY BOCK

Tempo di Valse

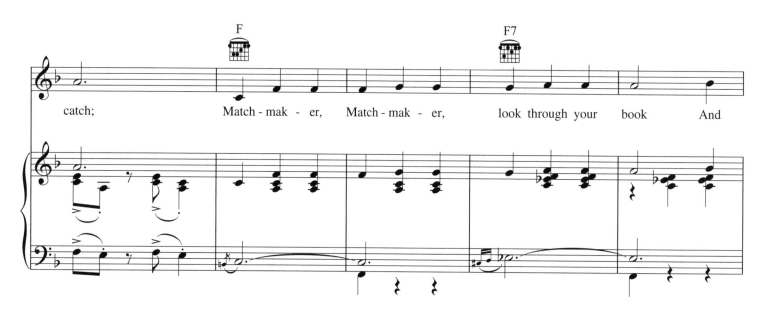

SABBATH PRAYER
from the Musical FIDDLER ON THE ROOF

Words by SHELDON HARNICK
Music by JERRY BOCK

Slowly, sincerely

May the Lord pro-tect and de-fend you, May He al-ways shield you from shame; May you come to be in Par-a-dise a shin-ing name. May you be like Ruth and like Es-ther.

SHE LOVES ME
from SHE LOVES ME

Words by SHELDON HARNICK
Music by JERRY BOCK

SUNRISE, SUNSET
from the Musical FIDDLER ON THE ROOF

Words by SHELDON HARNICK
Music by JERRY BOCK

'TIL TOMORROW
from the Musical FIORELLO!

Words by SHELDON HARNICK
Music by JERRY BOCK

Gently

Twi-light de-scends, ev-'ry-thing ends 'til to-mor - row, _____ to-mor - row. Since we must part, here is my heart 'til to-mor - row, _____ to-

TONIGHT AT EIGHT

from SHE LOVES ME

Words by SHELDON HARNICK
Music by JERRY BOCK

TOO CLOSE FOR COMFORT
from the Musical MR. WONDERFUL

Words and Music by JERRY BOCK,
LARRY HOLOFCENER and GEORGE WEISS

Passionately

wise, be smart, be-have, my heart. Don't up-

set your cart when {she's} {he's} so close. __

Be soft, be sweet, but

be dis-creet. Don't go off your beat. {She's} {He's} too

WHEN DID I FALL IN LOVE
from the Musical FIORELLO!

Lyrics by SHELDON HARNICK
Music by JERRY BOCK

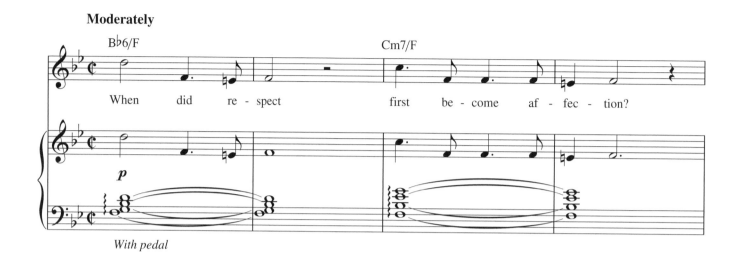

When did re-spect first be-come af-fec-tion?

When did af-fec-tion sud-den-ly soar?

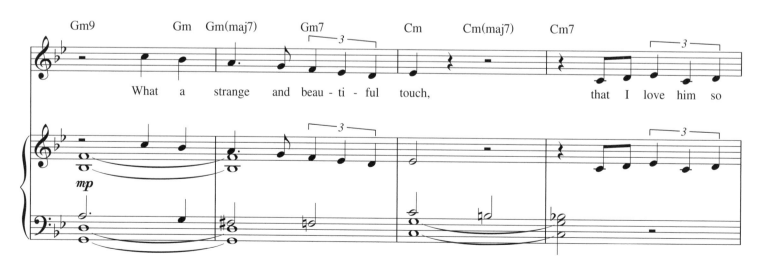

What a strange and beau-ti-ful touch, that I love him so

WILL HE LIKE ME?

from SHE LOVES ME

Words by SHELDON HARNICK
Music by JERRY BOCK

Moderately slow   AMALIA:

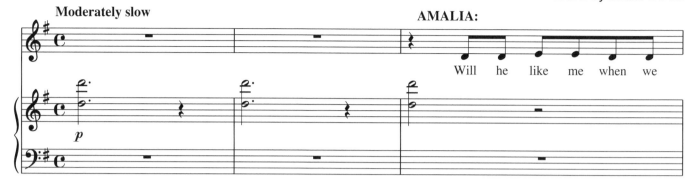

Will he like me when we

meet? _____ Will the shy and qui-et girl he's going to see _____ Be the

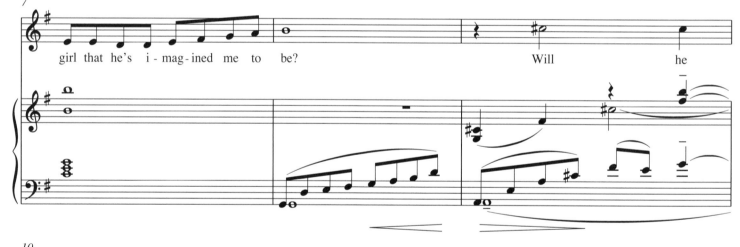

girl that he's i-mag-ined me to be? Will he

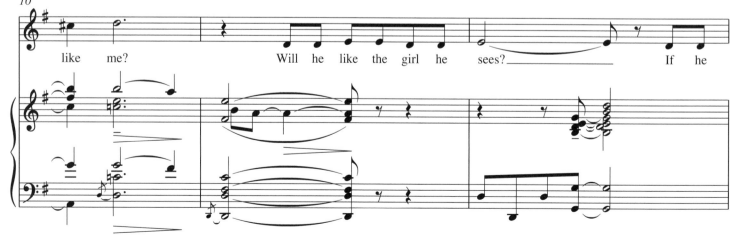

like me? Will he like the girl he sees? _____ If he

Broaden

pen. _____ Will he know that there's a world of love

wait - ing to warm him? How I'm hop - ing that his eyes and

ears won't mis - in - form him. Will he like me? I don't

a tempo

know. _____ All I know is that I'm tempt-ed not to go. _____ It's in -

san - i - ty for me to wor - ry so. I'll try

not to. Will he like me?

He's just got to. Will he like me?

Very slowly

Will he like me?

VANILLA ICE CREAM
from SHE LOVES ME

Words by SHELDON HARNICK
Music by JERRY BOCK